Aaron and Gayla's Counting Book

written by Eloise Greenfield

pictures by Jan Spivey Gilchrist

1 2 3

1

One fat raindrop bouncing on the window.
One boy ringing a doorbell.

Two children almost ready to play in the rain.

2

3

Three boots.

Four boots.

4

5 Five steps to walk down.

Six clouds spilling soft rain.

6

7

Seven people walking fast.

Eight trees dripping.

8

9 Nine puddles to splash in.

Ten wet tulips.

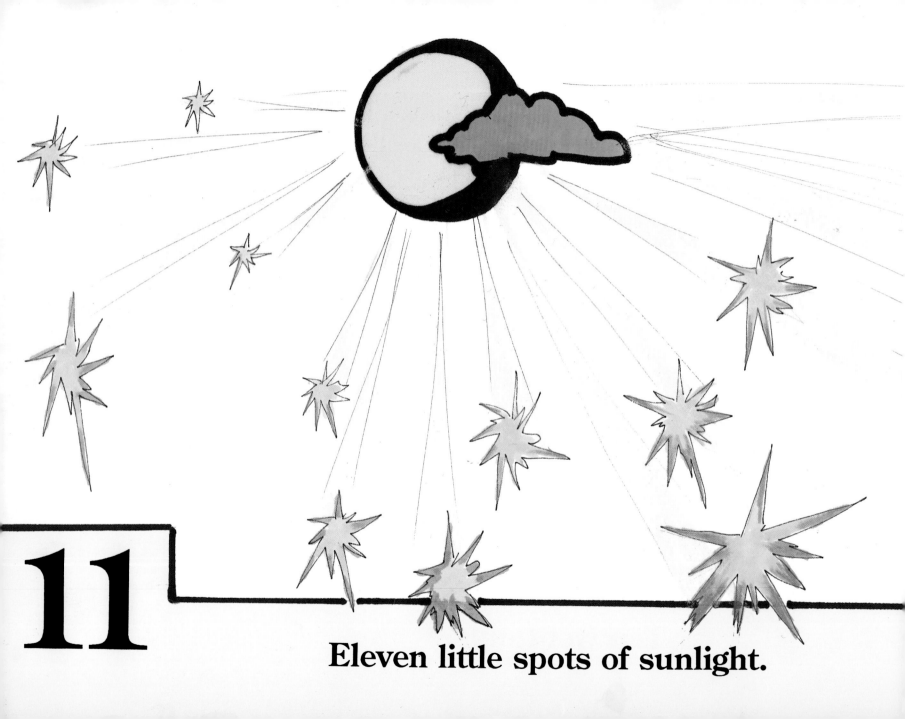

11

Eleven little spots of sunlight.

Twelve birds shaking their feathers.

12

13

Thirteen umbrellas starting to dry.

Fourteen stones drying in the sun.

14

15

Fifteen windows shining.

Sixteen children coming out to play.

16

17

Seventeen bushes trembling in the wind.

Eighteen green leaves blowing in the wind.

18

Nineteen children looking at the sky.

19

Twenty hard raindrops chasing the children home.

20

We're marching in the rain,
We're marching in the rain,
The music makes a beat,
Just like our stamping feet, *count,*

1	2	3	4
one	two	three	four
5	6	7	8
five	six	seven	eight
9	10	11	12
nine	ten	eleven	twelve
13	14	15	16
thirteen	fourteen	fifteen	sixteen
17	18	19	20
seventeen	eighteen	nineteen	twenty

Marching in the rain, yeah!
Marching in the rain, yeah!
Marching in the rain, yeah!

We're marching in the rain!